Hercules *and the* Golden Apples

Introduction

Long ago, people told stories called myths. The characters were often gods and heroes. One purpose of the myth was to explain things in nature that people did not understand. *Hercules and the Golden Apples* is a myth from ancient Greece that has been rewritten as a drama. As characters act out the drama on stage, the story comes to life for the audience.

Characters

VILLAGER	KING
HERCULES	KING'S ATTENDANT
NEREUS	PROMETHEUS
ATLAS	NATURE SPIRITS

Scene One
The Task

In ancient Greece, a powerful hero stands before a king. A man from the nearby village walks onto the stage and addresses the audience.

VILLAGER: Who has not heard of the strength of Hercules? Long ago, Hercules used that strength in terrible ways because of a curse the goddess Hera put on him. When he realized what he had done, he asked the gods for forgiveness. Hercules wanted to earn back his honor so the gods sent him to work for a king. The king decreed that Hercules must complete twelve tasks. Despite all odds, Hercules completed ten difficult tasks. Now it was time for Hercules to learn what his eleventh task would be.

KING: I want three of Hera's golden apples! Get them and bring them to me!

HERCULES: Each task has been difficult. But I fear that this one may be impossible.

VILLAGER: Now, the king knew that getting Hera's apples was likely an impossible task. But the king didn't like Hercules and secretly hoped that he would fail.

KING: *(laughing)* Impossible, you say? Let's just say *challenging*!

HERCULES: But Hera's shining apples are made of gold and have special powers. The goddess loves her apple tree above all else. It is planted in a secret garden and no one has ever been able to find it!

KING: *(nodding)* All true. It is also said that three nature spirits guard the tree. A dragon with many heads lives at the foot of the tree, too. But you are clever and strong, Hercules! I'm sure you can figure out what to do.

VILLAGER: Could Hercules get past the nature spirits and the dragon? Maybe, if he was clever enough. But none of that would matter if he could not even *find* the apple tree! Hercules walked away feeling the heavy weight of failure.

KING'S ATTENDANT: *(steps out from behind a shrub)* Hercules, I can help you. But do not tell the king that I did so.

HERCULES: How can you help me?

KING'S ATTENDANT: *(whispering)* Find Nereus, the old man of the sea. He knows where Hera's apple tree can be found.

The Journey

Hercules arrives at the seashore and waits for Nereus to appear.

VILLAGER: Hercules hoped that the words of the king's attendant would bear fruit. He knew this could be his only chance to learn the location of Hera's apple tree.

HERCULES: *(quietly to himself)* What's that sound? Is that Nereus I hear?

NEREUS: *(appearing on a wave and singing)* The sea is deep, dark, and cold. The sea holds secrets, new and old.

HERCULES: *(grabbing Nereus)* Aha! I have you! Tell me where to find Hera's golden apples!

VILLAGER: Nereus began to change shapes, hoping to slip through the strong arms of Hercules. But Hercules held tight.

HERCULES: *(stubbornly)* Has the cat got your tongue, Nereus? Speak to me! Tell me the location of Hera's apple tree!

NEREUS: *(singing)* I am Nereus, the old man of the sea. Hera's secret is safe with me!

VILLAGER: Hercules was as strong as an ox and he did not let go. After a while, Nereus realized that he could not escape. He told Hercules where to find Hera's apples. Nearby, someone else was listening. Prometheus, a god who had been chained to a rock, heard everything.

PROMETHEUS: *(groaning)* Hercules! I beg your help!

VILLAGER: After losing an argument with another god, Prometheus had been chained to a rock. Every day, an eagle appeared and pecked at the god. Hercules felt sorry for him.

HERCULES: *(breaking the chains)* You are free now, Prometheus!

PROMETHEUS: Hercules, for your kindness, I will tell you something that will save your life. I know that you are on your way to pick Hera's apples. But only a god can pluck the apples from Hera's tree and live.

HERCULES: Thank you for telling me this, Prometheus! Will you go with me then?

PROMETHEUS: I am sorry, but I cannot go. Perhaps you will meet another god on your way to the tree.

HERCULES: Perhaps I will.

VILLAGER: Now that Hercules knew where the tree was located, he felt better about his chance of success. Yes, he needed to get past the nature spirits and the dragon. And, yes, he needed to find a god who would pick the apples for him. But Hercules knew that he was both strong *and* clever. And, perhaps, luck would be on his side.

Atlas and the Trick

Hercules reaches the garden where Hera's tree grows. A gentle breeze rustles its leaves. On a nearby hill, Hercules sees the god Atlas, who has been forced to hold the world on his shoulders. Hercules gets an idea.

HERCULES: Atlas, if you will pick three apples from Hera's tree for me, I will hold the world for you.

VILLAGER: Now, Atlas quickly agreed because it was hard work to hold the heavy world on his shoulders.

ATLAS: I will pick the apples for you, but first you must kill the dragon under the tree.

VILLAGER: Hercules drew his bow and shot the beast. Then he took the world from Atlas. As Atlas approached the tree, the nature spirits begged and cried.

NATURE SPIRITS: *(together)* You can't take the apples! We beg you! Hera will return soon! She will be so angry!

ATLAS: *(shaking his head)* She will be angry with *you,* but not with me. I will be far away by the time Hera returns!

HERCULES: *(upon seeing Atlas with the three apples)* You've done it! Thank you, Atlas!

ATLAS: *(laughing)* Don't thank me! I won't be taking the world back from you!

VILLAGER: Now Hercules had thought this might happen, so he was ready.

HERCULES: Oh, Atlas, you have tricked me! Now you will have to take the apples to the king. As for me, I will be carrying this heavy world forever!

ATLAS: *(pleased with himself)* Yes, it was a good trick!

HERCULES: Could I ask just one favor before you leave? This world is heavy and hard. I would like to make a pad for my shoulders. Will you hold the world while I make the pad?

VILLAGER: Atlas agreed to this. He placed the apples on the ground and took the world again. As soon as he did so, Hercules grabbed the apples and hurried off.

ATLAS: *(shouting)* Hercules, come back!

HERCULES: I am sorry, Atlas, but I have to take the apples to the king! I am sure you understand!

A Task Completed

Hercules appears before the king with the three golden apples.

KING: *(surprised)* But, how did you find the tree? How did you get past the nature spirits and the dragon? This task was all but impossible!

HERCULES: *(proudly)* As you said before I left, it was a challenging task, but not impossible.

KING: *(fearfully)* Hera will be so angry with us. I cannot take the apples, Hercules. Let's ask the goddess Athena to return them to her.

VILLAGER: The king called for Athena who agreed to return the apples.

HERCULES: That completes task eleven. I am now but one task away from gaining forgiveness from the gods!

KING: Indeed you are, Hercules. Indeed you are. I will go now and think about task twelve.

VILLAGER: As the king walked away, Hercules sighed. He knew that the king would make sure that his last task would be the most difficult one yet. Would he succeed? Only time would tell.

Respond to Reading

Summarize

Use important details to summarize what happens in *Hercules and the Golden Apples.*

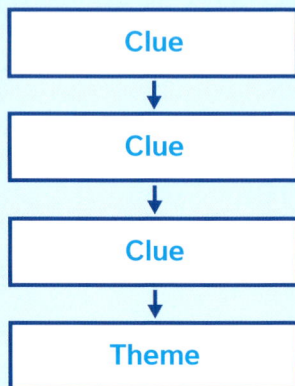

Clue
Clue
Clue
Theme

Text Evidence

1. How do you know *Hercules and the Golden Apples* is a drama? Genre

2. What is the overall idea this drama tells about? Theme

3. Use sentence clues to figure out the meaning of *tasks* on page 3. Sentence Clues

4. Write about why Hercules was looking for Hera's golden apples. Write About Reading

Compare Texts

Read about real apples.

Apples

Apples grow on trees all over the world. Apples can be red, yellow, or green. They can taste sweet or tart.

This tree grows Golden Delicious apples.

A group of apple trees is called an orchard.

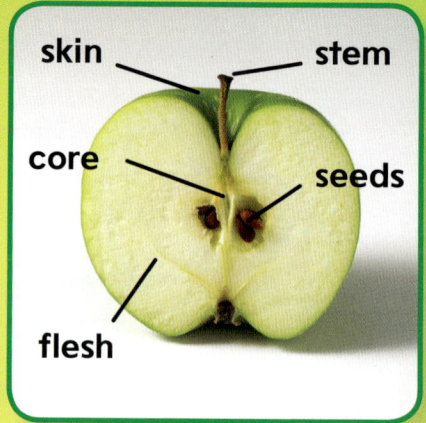

skin

stem

core

seeds

flesh

Look at the different parts of an apple.

An apple grows in stages. First, a bud forms on the tree. In spring, the bud blooms into a flower. Part of the flower will develop and grow into an apple.

Most apples are grown from a process called grafting. A farmer follows steps:

1. Cut a bud from a tree.
2. Make a cut in the bark of another tree.
3. Peel back the bark's edge.
4. Put the bud's stem under the bark.
5. Tape the bud and bark together.

Apples are a healthful snack.

People have eaten apples since prehistoric times. Apples probably grew first in Southwest Asia. Colonists brought apples with them to America. They are one of the world's favorite crops.

Today, China grows the most apples, and the United States is the second-biggest apple grower. The United States grows about 5 million tons of apples per year.

Make Connections

What can we learn from the myth of Hercules? **Essential Question**

How are real apples different from Hera's apples? **Text to Text**

Focus on Genre

Drama A drama is a story that can be acted out on stage. The story is told through dialogue that characters speak. Different scenes tell where the action takes place and what happens.

What to Look for *Hercules and the Golden Apples* is a myth told as a drama. Hercules is a hero who shows how strong and clever he is. Atlas is a god who holds the world on his shoulders. In one scene, the dialogue between Atlas and Hercules shows how they trick each other. Stage directions tell how Atlas speaks his words after he tricks Hercules.

Your Turn

Plan your own drama about a god, goddess, or hero from long ago. Give your character a name and tell what powers he or she has. Write where the story takes place and what your character needs to find or do.